21 Days to More Sales for Authors

Julia A. Royston

BK Royston Publishing
P. O. Box 4321
Jeffersonville, IN 47131
http://www.bkroystonpublishing.com
bkroystonpublishing@gmail.com

© Copyright – 2016

All Rights Reserved. No part of this book may be reproduced, stored in a retrieval system, or transmitted by any means without the written permission of the author.

Cover Design: Vikiana

ISBN: 9780981813530

Printed in the United States of America

Dedication

This book is dedicated to all of the authors who I have met on their journey to being a published author.

I also dedicate this book to all of the BK Royston Publishing and Royal Media and Publishing current and future authors. Let's go get it!

Acknowledgements

I would like to acknowledge my Lord and Savior Jesus Christ who has given me the gift and creativity to write.

To my husband who always has my back and a critical eye and ear for whatever project I undertake. Thank you sweetie, I love you.

To my girl, my coach, my ace, my best friend, Vanessa Collins who pushes me every day to be a better Publisher, Coach and Entrepreneur. Thank you and I love you.

To my family, you are the best!

To all of the authors who will purchase this book, go get that money! Let's go!

Love you all,

Julia A. Royston

Introduction

As a best-selling Author and Publisher, I am asked repeatedly by new authors how and where to sell and/or increase sales of their books. Instead of individually giving out this information, I have compiled 21 ways in 21 days to increase book sales for authors. These are not all of the answers and ways to increase book sales. I am learning daily to remain open to my surroundings and the spirit to lead and guide me in business and life.

Please email me at roystonjulia@gmail.com to share your success stories with using any of these methods to increase your book sales.

I look forward to speaking with you and continually help you to increase the sales of your books.

Julia A. Royston

If you are interested in BK Royston Publishing, LLC publishing your next best-seller, visit https://talkwithroyston.com.

Day 1

Inventory

Having books in your possession at all times is rule number one for authors. You must have books to sell books. Running out of inventory cannot be an option for authors. When people find out that you are an author, they will ask, "Where can I get your book?" Sometimes people will want to see your book and that is fine; however, the possible is greater when people see that you have books on hand. To have the money to purchase books, keep a portion of the profits from your books for more books. Your book is your product and your product is key to your profits. Keep your own inventory.

Challenge: How many books do you have in your inventory right now? How many books have you sold? What is your sales goal for the week, month or year?

_____
_____
_____
_____
_____
_____
_____
_____
_____
_____
_____
_____
_____
_____
_____
_____

Day 2

Tell Others

If people do not know that you have a book, they can't buy it. This sounds so basic, but in my experience with publishing other author's books, this is one of the keys to not making sales. I have often asked authors a specific question, "Have you told anybody about your book?" Their answer was "no." I can guarantee you that their book won't sell more than a few.

Being an author, you have to get over the shyness, awkwardness or resistance to let others know that you have written a book. They can't buy or support something they don't know about. Tell others that you have written a book. Tell your family and friends and let them help you tell others about your book.

Challenge: For the next 21 days, challenge yourself to tell one new person that you are an author and have a published book. Try to make a connection with the individual person and their interest if necessary, but make an effort to let others know about your book.

_____
_____
_____
_____
_____
_____
_____
_____
_____
_____
_____
_____
_____
_____

Day 3

Sales/Street Team

Word of mouth is still the best advertisement. My business has grown significantly because of word of mouth advertising. People who have actually utilized my services and were happy told others. Use this same premise but on purpose and strategically and recruit a "street team."

If you have an electronic version and final draft pre-printed copy of your book, recruit people that you know and trust to read the book. After they have read the book, then ask that they tell their social media followers or post a review online for you to link to and share their experience with your book. Don't forget to provide a link for others to buy your book!

If the street team member sells a physical book, they should receive a portion of the profits from that sale. Even though they didn't write the book but benefit from each sale. It will help you sell more books. The old saying, "More hands, less work" is especially true in books sales.

Challenge: Who do you know that supports you regardless of the project, product or event that you are involved? They should be a member of your street team. Make a list and get started.

Day 4

Buy or Pay Link

This sales strategy seems almost ridiculous to mention, but it is so true. Authors get so excited about posting their book covers and notifying others that they have the book, they forget to post the buy or pay now link. How are people going to buy the book if they don't have a button to click on? Their comments and likes don't equal money in your account. The button that takes them to a buy now or pay link and enter their credit card puts money in your account. Always post a buy or pay link wherever you post your book's cover. Make the amount of clicks the person has to click as few as possible. The person should not have to go deep into a site or click more than 3 times to get to the buy or pay button.

If you are posting your book cover on another site, indicate where the potential buyer can buy the book like Amazon.com,

Barnes&Noble.com, www.mydomain.com.
Don't forget the pay button!

Challenge: List all of the places that your book can be sold with the links to the **buy or pay** button. Create a shortened URL to make access even quicker to buy your book. Test out the **pay or buy** button BEFORE you post it. See how many clicks it takes to buy your book.

_____
_____
_____
_____
_____
_____
_____
_____
_____
_____
_____
_____
_____

Day 5
Online Distribution for Your Book

As a publisher, I encourage my authors to have as many distribution outlets as possible, including online distribution. I realize that there is a great debate about the online distributors, their payment methods, fees and how royalties are distributed but, what is the alternative? Yes, you could sell the book one at a time yourself through your website. On the other hand, the bottom line alternative to online distribution is limited access to the world's buyers of your book. The alternative is taking much longer to bring awareness to your book via your website or social media. Although your personal website can be accessed anywhere in the world, people have to know about your site to gain access to your book. The

International sites have that reputation and customers that can potentially land you in the same search results as a New York bestselling author's book.

I realize that some authors are more concerned with the profit margin rather than the accessibility of their book. In the end, you limit your access to buyers by not having online distribution outlets. Online distributors such as Amazon.com, Barnes&Noble.com, Kobo or other online distributors have fees, pay only quarterly, but whether you are self-published or signed with a company, these outlets collect the fees and payments, and they also mail the book directly to the customer. It is the price of doing business. If you do not have your books on these online distribution outlets, you literally have to do the work yourself, one book at time, one customer at a time. It's your choice. Which would you choose?

Challenge: Where can buyers buy your book online? Have as many outlets to purchase your book as possible and do not exclude the larger online distribution websites.

_____
_____
_____
_____
_____
_____
_____
_____
_____
_____
_____
_____
_____
_____
_____

Day 6
Your Own Website

The greatest profit margin for your book will be made when you sell your book from your website. The only thing you have to remember is that you are responsible for the book arriving safely into the hands of your reader. If there are any problems with delivery, like the wrong address or if their current address changes, you are still responsible for delivery.

When you create your own website, make sure the URL, the address created to access your website, is void of odd spellings, spaces or unnecessary characters. Your website needs to be memorable and easy to find. In addition, once people access your website, they will want to navigate quickly to the appropriate pages.

Place the book that is available for purchase on the front page and not embedded within several pages or clicks on your website. Once the reader clicks on the book cover, it should take them directly to a payment system immediately. Saves the reader time because you only have a short window to grab their attention and entice them to pay. Too many clicks to navigate to the pay page can result in a loss of the sale.

Challenge: Set up a basic website for yourself or your book. Purchase the domain and begin selling your book immediately. Write the URL or address for your website in the space provided below. One more thing that you can mark off of your to-do list.

_____
_____
_____
_____
_____
_____
_____
_____
_____
_____
_____
_____
_____

Day 7

Blogging

There are so many free blogging sites out there it's not funny. Start blogging about topics surrounding your book. Make your book available on your blog. Market and promote your blog on your other social media sites. There are bloggers looking for guest bloggers to speak to their audiences which increases your reach and introduces you to a new audience. Always make sure that you embed your book cover permanently on the front page or blog for ease of access and positioning for purchase. Don't forget the pay link when you click on the book cover.

Be consistent with your blog. If you post once a month, stick to a schedule. If you post once a week, do that consistently. People will be looking for your posts. When you change from that set schedule, there is a possibility to lose followers and potential customers.

Blog about what you are passionate about because it will make it easier to keep up the entries.

Challenge: First, conduct a search on blogs about your book topic, passion, or business. Start following their blogs. Read the entries and discover what their followers like to read about. Scroll to the bottom of the front page of a blog that you follow and determine where the blog is hosted or what website powers the blog. Reach out to the owner of the blog and ask about the ease of use and set-up of the blog using this hosting site. If you get a positive review about the ease of use, sign-up with that company and Start blogging!

_____
_____
_____
_____
_____
_____
_____
_____

Day 8

Media

Media attention whether traditional radio, internet radio or tradition television allows an author a wider reach to an audience rather than one at a time. Given that most traditional television stations pre-record all of their programs, you cannot only their live viewing audience, but their online audiences as well. Imagine the potential sales if you advertise in front of these audiences. In addition to the increased visibility of your book, but if the topic is extremely relevant, resonating with the audience, your chances of making those sales increase as well.

Simple, right? Not really, but very possible. You have to be ready for media on any level, but with your book listed on your website and online distribution sites in place, reach out and pitch your book to the media. Television personalities provide contact information directly on the screen as they report the news or during the course of their programming; whereas, radio personalities provide their contact information on their perspective websites. You won't know until you go for it.

Challenge: Make a list of the local radio and television stations within your immediate viewing area, including all pertinent contact information. Send each of them your book cover, your bio and a request to be a guest on their show. You never know what could happen. Remember the news comes from the community. You have written a book. That's the hottest news out there...

_____
_____
_____
_____
_____
_____
_____
_____
_____
_____

Day 9

Live Events

In my experience, I have sold the most of any product that I have to offer at live events such as conferences, workshops, trade shows or outside festivals. The personal interaction with potential readers increases your recognition and helps customers feel more connected to you as a writer; thusly, they will be more likely to purchase your book.

When appearing at live events, make sure that you have enough inventory. Make sure you have plenty of change available for cash payments and that you can also accept electronic payments. Make your display table and surrounding environment inviting. If you have an upcoming event or new book to promote, hand out cards, flyers or brochures. Even if you don't make a sale, offer a "give-away" of some kind related to your book, product or service. Make sure that you have a way to collect email addresses and contact information obtained from customers and other event attendees. This information is important to remain in contact for future book releases, events and other services that you offer. Create a simple sign-up sheet with two columns for their name and email address attached to a clip board with an ink pen is sufficient to start to gather this information.

Live events for an author are as critical to sales as a politician needing to meet people and be seen doing it by the media. You make a direct connection with the public. These are your potential customers. Be sure to shake hands, give them a smile and find a way to draw attention to you and your book. It could lead to a book sale.

Challenge: Locate at least 5 live events that attract your audience and potential clients.

_____
_____
_____
_____
_____
_____
_____
_____
_____
_____
_____
_____
_____
_____
_____

Day 10
Strategic Partnerships

Relationships are critical to any endeavor. You can always get more accomplished with help by a group, team or partnership. In my experience, you have to be strategic, careful and cautious with whom you partner with. Why? Because the people you associate with are a reflection of you, your character and your behavior, if you do not combine forces with an organization or an individual that is committed to providing similar services, you could end up exhausted and burned out.

First, find partnerships that are mutually beneficial. Second, have a written agreement regarding the terms of your partnership. Verbal agreements can be vague, causing friction and confusion, especially if one party seems to benefit more than the other party. Be sure to make the terms of the agreement clear and definitive. If you agree to a one year partnership, stick with that. If you agree to a long term partnership, but require a 30 day written notice to get out of the agreement, hold to your agreement.

Finally, do not partner for the sake of partnering. Make sure that the people you choose as partners have the same goals, speak to the same audiences, and offer complementary products and services.

Challenge: Find an organization to partner with, whether it be private or public, a nonprofit, or a government agency that will assist with your book sales. Even though you will take some risks partnering up with others, determine that the benefits of that partnership outweighs any risk involved.

_____
_____
_____
_____
_____
_____
_____
_____
_____
_____
_____
_____
_____
_____
_____
_____
_____
_____

Day 11

Government Contracts

The U. S. Government is the largest employer of people. According to the website, www.federaljobs.net, the U. S. Government employs more than 2.1 million people a year. Should you go get a job with the federal government? If you desire to, but you may wish to subcontract through a governmental agency. There are opportunities especially for women, minorities and veterans. If you do not want to go through the paperwork of being a certified subcontractor for the government, consider being a subcontractor for someone who is a certified subcontractor and can use your book as a textbook and training tool. Are you a certified trainer and have a skill or expertise that the government is looking for? Great. Write that book and sell your training services along with your book for increased sales.

Challenge: Contact your local or state Small Business Association or visit www.sba.gov to find out more about the steps necessary to become a certified contractor.

Day 12
Speaking Engagements

You sell when you speak. It's as simple as that. I have never been a speaker, facilitator, featured singer or done any other type of performance that somebody did not ask me about my books, my music or my business. It's a proven fact. Some of you have never participated in a speaking engagement and might wonder how to go about doing so. Below are some helpful hints to guide you in the right direction.

"First, check out local organizations, schools, social clubs, and nonprofits who often look for speakers to support their events. Make sure what you have to offer complements their forum, while at the same time, allows you to present your work as well. I would recommend you don't charge for speaking engagements if you are just starting out. The exposure itself is compensation enough until you create a reputation for yourself through successful speaking evens and positive reviews of your work."

Secondly, it is important to always present yourself in a positive light. I don't care how much information you know, if you aren't nice, pleasant, and helpful, people will not listen to what you have to say. First impressions do matter, and if you come off rude and dismissive, you might lose potential customers for both present and future endeavors."

Lastly, a successful speaker organizes his/her discussion points, making sure they are content rich, passionate, and relatable to the audience. In addition, I recommend utilizing a sign-up sheet to collect contact information from audience members and handing out business cards. After the speaking event, reach out to those who gave contact information, thanking them for coming to support your work. Add those contacts to your future communications about upcoming events, books, blogs, etc. that may interest them."

Challenge: Conduct an online search for organizations in your area looking for speakers, including networking groups, business networks, companies, schools and other organizations related to your book. Reach out to them and pitch your book and your talk.

_____
_____
_____
_____
_____
_____
_____
_____
_____
_____
_____
_____

Day 13
VIP Communication

Making connections and keeping connections are often two different things. Communication is key in any relationship. As an author with a book to sell, regardless of the venue, you must communicate effectively to those people who are genuinely interested in you and your passion. It doesn't matter whether you blog, have a monthly or quarterly newsletter, a private Facebook page or participate on another online group, reach out to your followers to make them feel special through personal emails, pre-recorded videos, or teleconferences. Make VIP Communication a priority with your readers and followers. Give them something an exclusive offer when they buy your book. If a current reader or follower refers another person, you could offer prizes, gifts, or discounts for the referral.

This creates a "team" mentality and encourages your readers to advertise for you because they benefit from that support. Remember, VIP stands for, "Very Important Person," and so you should treat them as such.

Challenge: Make a list of possible VIP communication methods you would be interested in starting. Make sure you take into consideration the time and energy you would be willing to invest. What kinds of incentives would you offer to your VIP readers?"

_____
_____
_____
_____
_____
_____
_____
_____
_____
_____
_____

Day 14

Audio Book

Offering the book in another format **is** yet another way to increase sales of your book. In today's market, digital access to content **is** crucial. There **is** an entire new market for audio, digital and streaming content. People often multi-task while they are learning; therefore, they may find it more convenient to listen to your book as they participate in other activities. The more options you have, the better your chances of selling your books to a wider audience

Technology is so advanced that you can economically purchase headphones and a microphone to record directly into your computer. If you are inexperienced with this technology, I suggest that you contact a local recording studio to record your audio book by a professional. I record my audio books in my own voice. If you are uncomfortable doing this yourself, find someone with a wonderful speaking voice and pay them to record it for you. There is some expense involved but in the end, it will be worth it! Get started to more sales by having your book in audio format.

Challenge: Download an audio app and record the first chapter of your book on your phone. Listen to it and see how it sounds. Continue to record until the entire book is finished.

Day 15

Local Bookstores

In cities around the country, local bookstores strive to stay afloat. Many of them offer local authors space on their bookstore shelves as a way to support the community. In turn, those bookstores might request that you promote their businesses by sharing where people can purchase your book. It's a win, win situation. The local bookstore is promoted, your book is promoted and you obtain a broader audience which should lead to sales.

The local bookstore may charge a small consignment fee, but you have obtained a new distribution outlet, a wider audience of readers, and hopefully, an increase in sales, which the benefits far outweigh the cost of a small fee. There is possibly a new audience of readers to read your book and an increase in sales volume than before.

Challenge: Conduct a search of the local bookstores in your area. Call or visit the local stores themselves and speak with the manager regarding placing your books in their store. See what happens. If one says no, go on to the next store. Don't stop until you get that yes!

Day 16
Bundle Your Book

Just like the phone, cable and internet access is bundled, bundle your book along with other services that you offer. For a price, include your book, a coaching call and another audio product. For a conference or workshop registration, include a copy of your book for each attendee. Because each attendee will already have a copy of your book, the value added comes from your ability to teach from your book during the conference or workshop. In addition, you might be able to gain clients who wish to be coached, or even schedule additional speaking engagements. It is clearly a win, win situation.

Challenge: What companion product, service or event can accompany your book? Sit down and determine that offer today. Create a flyer with graphics that reflects that offer begin selling your book with the special offer included.

_____
_____
_____
_____
_____
_____
_____
_____
_____
_____
_____
_____
_____
_____

Day 17
Connect with the Calendar

Create ways to connect your book with different events or celebrations throughout the year. For example, if you have written an inspirational book, connect with the month of January because many people are looking for ways to start the New Year out right. If your book deals with love or issues of diversity, you may wish to connect with the month of February for Valentine's Day and Black History Month. If your book is more concerned with female concerns, you may wish to consider March for its focus on Women's History. Whatever the case, figure out which month best supports the theme of your book and use that relevance to better promote sales.

Challenge: Get a year-long calendar. Write in festivals, events, activities, celebrations and family gatherings that can relate to your book and sell, sell and sell!

_____
_____
_____
_____
_____
_____
_____
_____
_____
_____
_____
_____
_____
_____
_____

Day 18
Video or Digital Streaming

Video is the hottest and most powerful tool today in technology. From Periscope, Facebook Live and the video capabilities of any smart phone can turn you into a video superstar. The content that you deliver via video should relate directly to something in your book to increase sales. When organizing content for your video, take notes to help you keep track of your main talking points and anything else you wish to include. During your video presentation, make sure you include a link to your website where people can sign up for upcoming events and special offers, purchase a copy of your book, or link up to your blogs, Facebook page, Practice daily and then start. It doesn't have to be perfect, just powerful. It doesn't have to be polished, just passionate. Don't miss out on the opportunities of the digital revolution and especially the power of video.

Challenge: Open the camera app on your phone and record a short video introducing yourself to the world. Begin with your name and what you do to help the world be better. Start! Let's go!

_____
_____
_____
_____
_____
_____
_____
_____
_____
_____
_____
_____
_____
_____

Day 19

Book Reviews

Word of mouth is a very powerful advertising and sales tool. I have seen it in action with authors. When people tell others how good the book is, it causes a frenzy of purchases. Sometimes there even may be controversy surrounding the book. We have seen controversial books have tremendous sales because of the curiosity of people. Whatever the case, reviews create a buzz for people to want to read which can lead to an increase in book sales.

How do you get a review of your book?

First, you should encourage anyone who has read your book to post a review on his/her social media sites or on the online distribution sites, like Amazon or B&N.com. Second, recruit a review team to read a pre-printed version of your book. Have them post their reviews or allow their reviews to be on your website permanently and then give them VIP treatment at an event or think of some other creative way to replay them for this service. Finally, there are services online that charge for a review. Research those companies and double-check that you receive the type of review you are paying for.

Challenge: Contact people who you know to request a review of your book. Make a list of 5-10 people who support you and would be willing to read and review your book. These people can also be your reader "Street Team" to help you promote your book.

_____
_____
_____
_____
_____
_____
_____
_____
_____
_____
_____
_____
_____

Day 20
Advertisement

Companies spend millions of dollars each year to advertise during the breaks of television shows, radio shows, billboards, etc. You may or may not have the money to spend on this type of advertisement, but you should determine what outlets you could utilize for advertising that does fit within your budget

Regardless if you advertise in a local booklet for an event, through a postcard at a busy coffee shop, or as an ad in an online magazine or newsletter, getting the word out is key; if people aren't informed, they can't purchase your book or attend your events.

You are in the book business and advertising is a part of business. It's a must and not an option.

Run an ad on a public access television station. Some advertising is better than none. Make sure the avenues you utilize to advertise hit the right target market for your product or service. Young people may be your target audience but they may not have the cash to spend on your book. Advertise so that their parents/guardians/grandparents/aunts/uncles will want to buy the book for them.

Challenge: Look for outlets to advertise your book. Many events allow advertisements in the form of flyers, postcards, business cards, etc. inside "glam" or "swag bags." Go for it!

Day 21
Affiliate/Referral Program

In addition to strategic partnerships, many companies offer a discount on services through direct referrals. A referral or affiliate program is an expansion of your sales/street team. These programs are systematic ways to determine who did the referring and reward them for their referral.

For example, if any current client of mine refers another author to sign on and pay for services through my company, I offer a discount to that current client for future services, or I pay a "finder's fee" for the referral.

You can technologically track the referrals using a specific link or code on your website when someone purchases your book. Secondly, the person who purchases can submit a code when checking out that indicates who has referred them to purchase your book.

This program is very similar to the existing commission-based compensation plans utilized by companies for their employees. In many stores, the person who assists you with your purchases and rings you up gets compensation for the item or items you purchased. In the case of many cell phone companies, the employees earn extra commissions based upon "up-selling," or talking you into purchasing accessories, highlighted items of the month, or adding on new lines to existing contracts. If it works in these situations, why not try it yourself? It can work for you book sales as well.

Challenge: Offer an affiliate program on your website or social media for those who refer people to you and your book. Determine and include a system that will allow people to reference who referred them to your website to purchase your book.

_____
_____
_____
_____
_____
_____
_____
_____
_____
_____
_____
_____

About the Author

Julia Royston spends her days doing what she loves, writing, publishing, speaking about her why and motto, "Helping You Get Your Message to the Masses, Turn Your Words into Wealth and Be a Book Business Boss." Julia is the author of 150+ books, published 400+, recorded 3 music CDs and coached others to be published authors and business owners. She is the owner of five companies, a non-profit organization and the editor of the Book Business Boss Magazine.

To stay connected with Julia, visit www.juliaakroyston.com.

More Books by this Author

www.ingramcontent.com/pod-product-compliance
Lightning Source LLC
Chambersburg PA
CBHW051659090426
42736CB00013B/2452